Where is God?

Where is God?

A Theology for the Here and Now

Volume One:
An Introduction to Basic Concepts

ANDY ROSS

RESOURCE *Publications* · Eugene, Oregon

WHERE IS GOD? A THEOLOGY FOR THE HERE AND
NOW
Volume One: An Introduction to Basic Concepts

Resource Publications
An Imprint of Wipf and Stock Publishers
199 W. 8th Ave., Suite 3
Eugene, OR 97401

www.wipfandstock.com

PAPERBACK ISBN: 978-1-5326-5880-8
HARDCOVER ISBN: 978-1-5326-5881-5
EBOOK ISBN: 978-1-5326-5882-2

Manufactured in the U.S.A.   09/27/18

To Jonathan Murray for waking me up

Contents

Where is God in this Book?

Like a great starving beast
My body is quivering
Fixed
On the scent
Of
Light.

– *The Scent of Light* by Hafiz[1]

GOD WAS REVEALED TO me twenty years ago. Since then, I have dedicated my life to the study of spirituality, theology, and religion. This book is a part of that revelation. Just as we are finite expressions of the eternal, so too, these words are finite expressions of my experience of eternity.

God is everywhere to me. God moves in the myths and rituals of the world's religious traditions, God sings in the words of poets and musicians, and God reaches out to me through the wonder of creation. There are no words to describe the experience of God. Ideas are limited and will, therefore, only be able to hold a fraction of God's limitless reality. This being said, it is my intention to entertain the most extensive ideas possible. So, I offer you this book,

1. Ladinsky, *The Gift*, 90.

Volume 1, as an introduction to a theology for the *here* and *now*.

HERE AND NOW

A theology for the *here* and *now* embraces two realities. One, it must be a theology rooted in the eternal presence of God. God is eternal. Thus, we experience God as an eternal reality. All that we can know about God is available to us in this moment, *here* and *now*. A practical theology will bring us into harmony with God's eternal presence. God is not waiting for us "out there" in some future paradise. God is reaching out to us *here* and *now*.

Two, a theology for the *here* and *now* will consider all that we have come to know about creation and the human condition, both secular and spiritual. Theology is most expansive when it integrates the vast knowledge gained from the world's religious traditions and the sciences. The physical and social sciences do not entertain theories about ultimate reality. Understanding temporal reality, however, is indispensable to theology. A theology for the *here* and *now* takes into account all that we have come to know as a people. We can never fully grasp ultimate reality. We can, however, extend our reach as wide as possible.

CONTENT

This introduction will not exhaust the breadth of a theology for the *here* and *now*, nor is that the intention. We will begin with these five topics because they are fundamental to all future theological inquiries:

1. *Creation*–All that we know about God is mediated through creation. The web of existence is the foreground of God's creative impulse. Theology begins where we are in time and eternity.

2. *Suffering*–There is no more important area of theological inquiry than that of suffering. Finding God in our darkest hour is the greatest gift that a practical theology can offer.

3. *Religion*–Religion is the historical and cultural record of those who have engaged the question, "Where is God?" If we are to ask this same question, we must first understand what religion is and how it functions.

4. *My Life*–Theology is only as good as its practical application. If we cannot find God in our lives, we cannot find God.

5. *The End*–Death haunts us. But, it does not have to. Finding God means finding life, even in death.

Volume 1 is merely an introduction. It is my intention that these ideas will create the groundwork for an integrative systematic theology for the *here* and *now*. Theology is the never-ending pursuit of a deeper understanding of the spiritual experience. This book is neither the beginning nor the end of mine.

AND IT BEGINS

This book is the story of my experience of God as mediated through the theological process. I believe that God is present in these words, just as God is present within me as I write them.

You do not have to agree with all that I offer. I only ask that you listen. Read the text slowly and pay attention to the silent presence of the eternal. Please question the content of this introduction, but do not let the argument I present distract you from finding God in your own life.

"Where is God?" is a question that changes me each time I ask it. I believe that it will change you, too.

Where is God in Creation?

> In the beginning, when God created the heav-
> ens and the earth and the earth was without
> form or shape, with darkness over the abyss
> and a mighty wind sweeping over the waters.
> Then God said: Let there be light, and there was
> light.

–Genesis 1:1-3[1]

IN THE BEGINNING

THE BEGINNING IS ALWAYS *now*. This may seem a con-
tradiction considering that you have witnessed many
beginnings and all of them are in the past. Yet, if we are
to understand how God creates, we must first try and see
creation through God's eyes. God is the beginning (alpha)
and the end (omega), but God is also eternal. Thus, God
experiences the beginning and end from the same eternal
moment. From God's perspective, it is always the beginning (and, subsequently, the end).

1. All biblical quotes from the *New American Bible Revised Edition*.

The reason we typically do not experience life in this way is that we are distracted by the illusion of time. If we are to return to the beginning, when God created the heavens and the earth, we must first understand how this illusion works.

The Timeline

Most consider time a fundamental aspect of the lived experience. My life began at *this* point in time, I went to college at *this* point in time, and I got married at *this* point in time. We see ourselves as a dot moving along a timeline (Figure 1). What we do not realize is that the timeline is a tool invented by us in order to measure how objects change in relation to one another.

Figure 1:

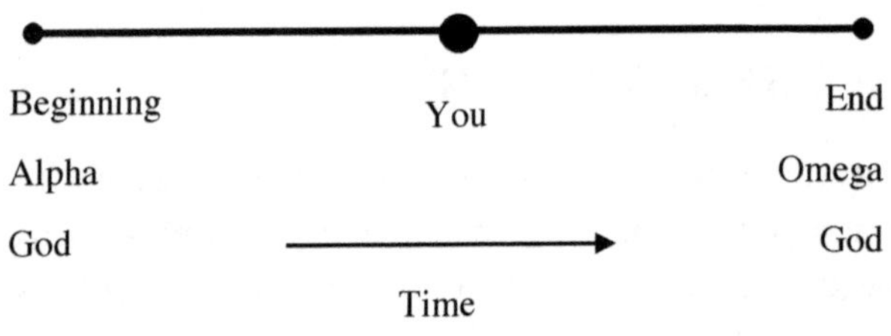

Beginning	You	End
Alpha		Omega
God	Time →	God

For example, the units of measurement on our timeline are days, months, years, etc. These units are based upon the rotation of the Earth on its axis (days), the phases of the moon (months), and the movement of the Earth around the sun (years). At the time I write this, the Earth has made its way around the sun 37 times, so we say that I am 37 years old.

The timeline is a highly beneficial tool of measurement. It helps us to understand the changes in our lives within the context of a larger environment. Every life form in existence is expanding and contracting, living and dying. By comparing our timeline to the timelines of other life forms, we are better able to appreciate our place within the hierarchy of life (i.e. my cat is 2 years old, I am 37 years old, and the earth is 4.5 billion years old). As long as we are utilizing the same timeline as those with whom we interact, we can make appointments, celebrate rites of passage, and measure the overall advancement of our species.

We live in a reality of change. The timeline helps us to live in accordance with that reality. But, it also limits our perspective.

The timeline is directional. It begins at point A (the birth of the life form in question), extends in one direction, and ends at point B (the death of the life form in question). Thus, we tend to view life as directional. I was born in the past (point A), I will die in the future (point B), and I exist as a dot somewhere in the middle.

Though this perspective is highly conducive to measuring change, it does not account for the cyclical nature of life. We measure life according to change. We experience life in cycles. There is another view of time that illustrates this.

Change is not only directional, it is also cyclical. Though our lives change progressively, in a linear fashion, change happens in cycles. We experience the same phenomena over and over, only from a different perspective. For example, it is summer again, but I am a year older. The timeline does incorporate cyclical elements–hours, days, and months repeat in order to coincide with the rotation and trajectory of the earth. A true cyclical view of time, however, goes a step further.

The Circle

If we were to view time as a circle (Figure 2), then life itself would be cyclical. Just as the end of one day is the beginning of another, the end of life is also a beginning. According to this view of time, life is ceaseless. Birth and death are united in the ongoing dance of creation.

Figure 2:

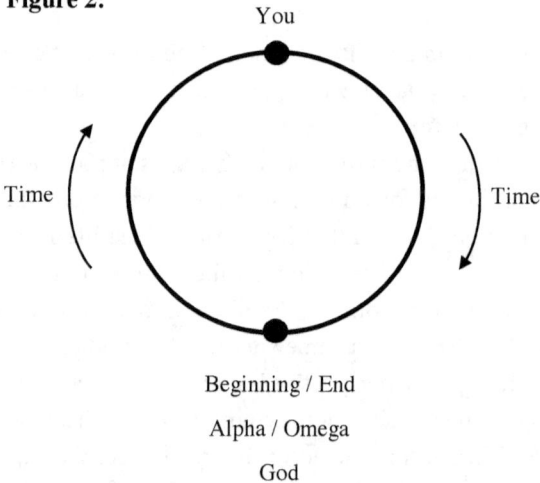

You

Time | Time

Beginning / End

Alpha / Omega

God

The cyclical view of time is prevalent in the Hindu traditions. *Samsara* is the cycle of birth, death, and rebirth. At the end of our life we return to *Brahman* (God) and then are reborn. The cycle lasts until we are able to liberate ourselves from it (*moksha*). Man, woman, tree, day, thought . . . each and every life form comes from God, lives, and then returns.

According to both the timeline (Figure 1) and the circle (Figure 2), we come from God, live, and then return to God. Yet, both concepts of time have their limitations. Though the timeline is more conducive to measuring change as a progression, it does not illustrate that if God is both alpha and omega (beginning and end) then beginning and end must be synonymous. The cyclical view of time helps us to shatter the illusion that life and death are somehow at odds, but it does not shatter the illusion of time itself. As long as we are a dot moving through time, we will never be able to view life as God does, from eternity.

ETERNITY

In the book of Genesis, God creates the first human in an act of breathing. "Then the LORD God formed the man out of the dust of the ground and blew into his nostrils the breath of life, and the man became a living being" (2:7). According to this image, our lives are animated by the breath of God.[2] Life expands as it is filled with God's being and then contracts as God draws it back in.

If you look around at the innumerable forms in creation, you will notice this pattern being repeated time and again. Life expands and contracts as the breath of God moves in and out of the formless void that is God's eternal being. In fact, many scientists believe that the universe itself is expanding, which seems to indicate that it will eventually contract. Time is what we use to measure the rate of this expansion (and contraction). Life changes as the breath of God animates it.

2. The Hebrew term for "breath of God" is *ruah*. The Latin translation is *spiritus*, which is where we get the term "spirituality."

God, however, does not change. God views the expansion and contraction of living forms from the same eternal moment. In fact, we all do.

God views life from the eternal *now*. And, though our minds are constantly interpreting the eternal *now* within the context of time (i.e. yesterday *this* happened, tomorrow I would like *this* to happen), *now* is all that exists. *Now* is the moment of eternal awareness. It is the single point of consciousness from which we view the changes in our lives. Life is expanding and contracting around our awareness of it. We are experiencing life from the same eternal moment as God. It is always the beginning and always the end, because it is always *now*.

In the Gospel of Thomas, Jesus said, "The Father's kingdom is spread out upon the earth, and people do not see it" (113:4).[3] The Father's kingdom is eternity. It is the eternal *now* from which God views creation. We typically do not see it because we are caught in the illusion of time. We believe that we are a dot moving along a timeline. The dot, however, does not move.

The Spiral

The spiral view of time illustrates the relationship between change and eternity (Figure 3). The dot at the center of the spiral represents the eternal moment from which God views the expansion and contraction of living things. This is the same moment from which we experience life. The dot is consciousness, both God's and ours. Life expands from God (the dot) in a circular motion (the spiral).

3. Meyer, *The Gnostic Gospels of Jesus*, 25.

Figure 3 (top view):

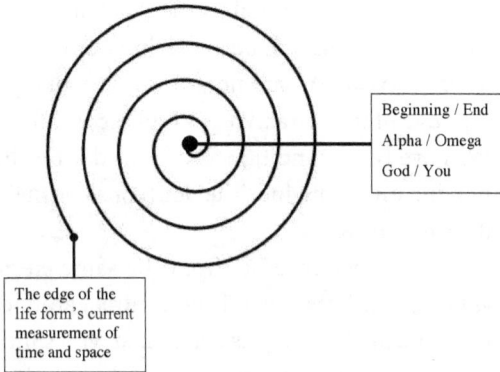

Beginning / End
Alpha / Omega
God / You

The edge of the
life form's current
measurement of
time and space

Figure 3 (side view):

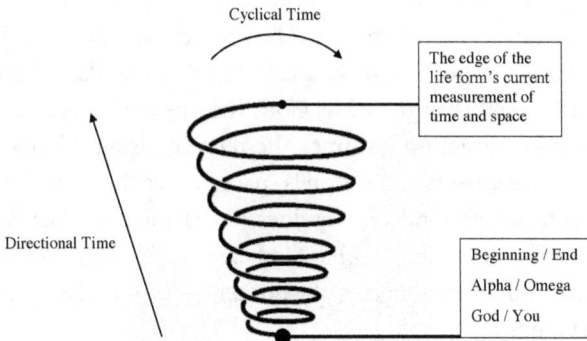

Cyclical Time

The edge of the
life form's current
measurement of
time and space

Directional Time

Beginning / End
Alpha / Omega
God / You

The image of the spiral opening upward illustrates the
directional momentum of life as well as its cyclical nature (the repetition of days, seasons, etc.). You could,
therefore, utilize the timeline or the circle to measure
the changes that take place as the life form expands. The

timeline would measure the rate of expansion in a directional sense, and the circle would measure time in cycles.

The outer edge of the spiral represents this moment as we experience it within the illusion of time. We typically consider *now* to be a certain hour of a certain day of a certain year. We are not, however, looking at life from the edge of the spiral. We are looking at it from the center. We have been conditioned to consider our lives as a dot moving on a timeline. The dot (consciousness), however, does not move.

We experience life from the same eternal moment as God. Our lives expand and contract around the eternal *now*. Spiritual practice is concerned with shifting our center of awareness from the edge of the spiral to the center, from an identification with change to an identification with God.

By altering our concept of time, we are better able to view creation from God's perspective: eternity. Yet, eternity is not just *now*, it is *here*. Life expands and contracts as it is animated by God. The rate of this expansion (and contraction) is time. The relative distance between various aspects of creation is space. Just as the eternal *now* from which God creates does not change, neither does God's orientation to what God creates. The *here* and *now* are both represented by the dot on the spiral view of time (Figure 3).

We are used to measuring space according to the position of our bodies in relation to other objects in creation. My body is in *this* location and your body is in *that* location. However, though our relative positions may differ according to the tool of measurement that we are using (inches, miles, light years, etc.), our experience of them originates in God's eternal being, the *here* and *now from* which all life expands and *to* which all life returns (the dot).

Eternity is *here* and *now*. Life simply changes around it (the spiral). By shedding our illusions of space and time, we are able to experience God's eternal presence. *Here* and *now*, we are able to view creation from God's eyes and discover the reason why God creates.

UN-MANIFEST

All "beings" that exist in temporal reality (the reality of created things) are manifestations of God's eternal being.[4] You and I are human beings, meaning we are human manifestations of being itself. We could, therefore, refer to a tree as a "tree being," a dog as a "dog being," and a star as a "star being." God's un-manifest reality is being without form, the eternal presence of God within and beyond creation. The un-manifest God is the alpha from which all forms arise and the omega to which they return.

God's un-manifest reality transcends creation. Therefore, it is the most difficult to comprehend. Our concepts are derived from experience, and our language from those concepts. God the father, God the mother, *ruah*, the light–each of these concepts stems from an experience of God within creation.

We are bound by concepts, and concepts are bound by experience. For this reason, the un-manifest God is often approached by juxtaposing positive and negative imagery (i.e., if manifest reality is form, un-manifest reality is formless or without form). By describing a

---

4. The breath of God (*ruah*) is God's being poured into creation.

phenomenon with which we are familiar, we are better able to comprehend its opposite.

Silence and Sound

Silence is not something that we can hear, nor is it a phenomenon that we can describe without utilizing its opposite. Silence is the absence of sound, the quiet from which sound arises and to which it returns.

Our experience of silence is similar to our experience of the un-manifest God. We experience creation as the rising and falling of temporal forms. Each of these forms (from molecules to humans to the universe itself) is an expression of God's eternal being. Beneath the movement of life, however, there is a silence. We experience this silence within creation, but somehow it is beyond it. Sound rises out of silence just as creation rises out of God's un-manifest reality. And, both inevitably return.

Silence is always present within and beyond sound. So, too, the un-manifest God is eternally present within and beyond creation. The dot in the spiral image of time is present whether the spiral exists or not. The dot simply is, just as God simply is.

But, why is there a spiral at all? What compels God to create? In the beginning (the eternal *here* and *now*) God empties itself into creation to fulfill a single desire: to know itself.

God's Desire

Being and consciousness (Sanskrit: *sat chit*) are two dimensions of God's un-manifest transcendence. The transcendent God is being without form and consciousness without forms to be conscious of. God cannot know itself in its eternity. Being and consciousness are a unified reality (being *is* conscious), beyond the capacity to be known.

Knowing requires duality. For there to be knowing, there must be a knower and a known, a subject and an object. In order for God to know itself, God must become the object of God's curiosity. Thus, God's single desire to know itself causes the unified ground of being to contract and divide (Hebrew: *tzimtzum*). As God turns within, God witnesses God, and the vast potentiality of being stretches forth as creation.

MANIFEST

Being itself is a boundless reality. In order for being to be known, it must be expressed as form. When God divides itself, God's eternal being is emptied into creation as a vibration that animates life. The manifest rises out of the un-manifest, like sound rising out of silence.

In the Hindu traditions, the sound of God creating is referred to as the sacred *aum*. As being *becomes*, its vibration expands outward, breaking the plane of manifest reality as form. Life moves as God's being moves within it. God is the eternal silence from which life expands (un-manifest transcendence), and God is the sound which animates it (manifest immanence). We are in God and God is in us.

All manifestations of God's being are expressed as form. And, forms expand as the vibration of God's being animates them. God as consciousness (knower) witnesses being's innumerable manifestations (known) from the eternal *here* and *now*. Life expands and contracts (the spiral) around God's awareness of it (the dot).

Using time as a tool of measurement however, we calculate that the universe has been expanding for 14 billion years. The mechanism for this expansion is two-fold: 1) God's eternal being emptied into creation, pushing it to expand and 2) the chain of causality: forms acting and reacting, resulting in a complexification of life moving outward toward self-actualization.

Life Expanding

A form expands as it is animated by God's being like a balloon being filled with air. The balloon (form) expands as the air (God's being/*ruah*) fills it. And, just as a balloon takes shape as it is filled, so too, a form becomes actualized as God's being animates it.

We witness this phenomenon in the rise and fall of life. From the tiniest molecule to the universe itself, all forms grow or expand as they are animated by God. The orientation and complexity of each form are determined by the potentialities already present. The initial forms created by God's self-emptying are direct expressions of the vibration of being *becoming* (*aum*). New potentialities are created by the interaction of forms, resulting in an increasing complexification of life.

Complexification

As forms expand, they do so towards a potential determined by internal and external factors. An oak tree will reach a certain height based upon the interaction of cells within it (internal factor), as well as its interaction with the environment (external factor).

Simultaneously, forms within and beyond the oak tree are expanding towards their potential (cells, other trees, earth, etc.). The oak tree exists within a hierarchy of expanding and contracting forms, comprising the interactive web of existence. As forms interact with one another, they do so in an environment fashioned by the interaction of previous forms. Thus, each form will have a greater potentiality than the previous, resulting in a greater potentiality for the hierarchy (i.e., an increasing complexification).

Self-Actualization

As the web of existence moves outward towards self-actualization, so do the forms within it. Self-actualization is the full expression of a form's potential as it is animated by God. Just as each expression of God takes on a specific form, each form has a unique character (or *self*). A form reaches self-actualization when God's being has been fully expressed through the various nuances of its character. Each form represents God's only opportunity to know itself as that form.

As a form expands, its *self* is more fully realized, allowing God the greatest opportunity for expression. God's desire to know itself is actualized through the creative process.

As we become, so does God.

GOD KNOWING GOD

We all experience life as knower/known (subject/object). I am the subject (knower) who witnesses the various objects (known) that come into my awareness. As forms expand and contract around me, I experience them as "other." Our experience of life as knower/known is what creates the illusion of duality. I am the subject (knower) who experiences the object (known); we are separate (dual).

Creation and the innumerable forms within it, however, are all manifestations of God's unified being. Thus, when I (knower) experience an object (known), God (knower) experiences God (known). On the surface, creation appears to be a hierarchy of individual forms expanding and contracting. In truth, this is all just God knowing God.

In the beginning God created the heavens and the earth. Heaven is *here* and the beginning is *now*. We are not the shadows of a creative act that took place billions of years ago. We are expressions of an eternal act of self-discovery *here* and *now*. God is breathing life into creation in this moment, and we, as expressions of God, are here to witness it.

Where is God in Suffering?

> It is hard to leave the world and hard to live in
> it, painful to live with the worldly and painful
> to be a wanderer. Reach the goal; you will wan-
> der and suffer no more.

−The Dhammapada Verse 302[1]

LIFE IS NOT AN easy journey. Although the act of being alive is joyous, the experience of living is complex and not always pleasant. There is, however, a lesson to be gleaned from pain and suffering and a theological approach to their existence. Our task in this chapter is to discover what might be gained from a deeper understanding of pain and suffering and, of course, how they relate to God.

Pain and suffering, though related, are two distinct phenomena. Pain is the inevitable rise of agitation in the body (physical and energetic) and is an unavoidable aspect of existing within a reality of form. Suffering, on the other hand, is the cycle of mental distress that stems from our desire for control.

By understanding the nature of both pain and suffering, we will be able to develop a more comprehensive

1. Easwaran, *The Dhammapada*, 213.

view of God and reality and may even be able to alleviate the latter all together.

THREE BODIES

Every manifestation of God's being is expressed in form, and each form experiences life through a body or bodies. "Body" refers to the form's specific vehicle, or vehicles, within which it navigates reality. I am a human being. I am, therefore, a unique form comprised of an interrelated set of bodies: a physical body, an energetic body, and a spirit body (Figure 4). Although there are no existential divisions between the three, dividing the body in this manner is beneficial, particularly to our understanding of pain.

Figure 4:

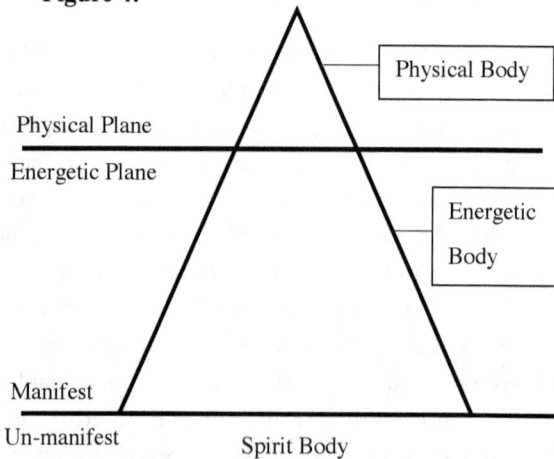

Physical Body

Physical Plane

Energetic Plane

Energetic Body

Manifest

Un-manifest

Spirit Body

Physical Body

On the surface, we seem to experience life as a physical body interacting with other physical bodies within a physical universe. The strength of this illusion is its obvious, though limited, truth. The physical body, whether my own body, the body of a tree, or the body of a proton, is the aspect of its expression that has taken physical form. If each form were an iceberg floating within the sea of God's being, the form's physical body would be the tip that protrudes from the surface.

We typically experience life via the five senses, and the five senses are each an apparatus of the physical body. We are, therefore, only able to recognize forms that are on the physical plane. The physical body is the most obvious vehicle through which we experience life. There are, however, two other bodies that support it.

Energetic Body

The second of the three interrelated bodies through which we experience life is the energetic body. The energetic body transcends and includes the physical body, meaning that the energetic body includes the physical body but is not limited to it. The vibration of God's being *becoming* creates and sustains life. When this vibration becomes manifest, it does so as energy.

All forms are energy. A form's physical body is merely the aspect of its energy which is discernable to the senses. Like the portion of an iceberg which lies beneath the surface, the bulk of the energetic body is indiscernible to the senses. Unlike the iceberg, however, the energetic body is much more malleable than the physical body. The energetic body shifts frequently and is highly susceptible to changes in the environment.

Energy is in constant motion, unlike the third body, which is absolute stillness.

Spirit Body

If the physical body is the tip of the iceberg and the energetic body is its submerged superstructure, the spirit body is water. The iceberg sits in water, is an expression of water, and is water. The spirit body is God's eternal being. As God's being (spirit) is poured into life, it breaks the energetic and physical planes. Thus, the spirit body includes both the energetic and physical bodies, but is limited to neither. The spirit body has no limitations. While the physical and energetic bodies are manifest, the spirit body is un-manifest. It has no beginning or end. Icebergs come and go. The water, however, remains.

PAIN

Pleasure and pain are not existentially distinct. They are merely separate interpretations of the same phenomenon: change. The physical and energetic bodies are constantly changing. The mind interprets these changes as either pleasurable or painful (in varying degrees). The interpretations are not arbitrary but are the result of the mind's ongoing evolution.

Typically, changes in the body that are considered beneficial are interpreted as pleasurable, and changes that are considered harmful are interpreted as painful. For instance, physical pain (pain arising in the physical body) is oftentimes the result of malfunction or injury. The mind interprets this change as painful in order to signify that a response is needed. On the other hand, resting is generally a pleasurable activity due to the body's need to recuperate.

While physical pain is the result of perceived shifts in the physical body, energetic pain (or emotional pain) is the result of perceived shifts in the energetic body. Elation, for instance, is an intense shift in the energetic body which is perceived as being highly beneficial.

My wife has been out of town for a week, and she surprises me by coming home a day early. My mind perceives the presence of my wife as highly beneficial. The energy in my body shifts to accommodate the environmental change (the presence of my wife), and I experience elation.

The sudden presence of a threat would be interpreted differently. Fear is the typical emotional response to a perceived threat in the environment. If I am walking down a dark alley and two hooded figures jump out from behind a parked car, my energetic body would shift due to my mind's interpretation of the change as dangerous.

Physical and energetic (emotional) pain are causally linked. The physical body is merely the aspect of the energetic body that can be perceived by the senses. Thus, changes in the energetic body cause changes in the physical body and vice versa. For example, both elation and fear can lead to increased heart rate and other physical changes.

The energetic body is much more malleable. The energy moving through our bodies is continuously responding to the energy around it. When you walk into a room where two people have been arguing, your emotional state changes. This is due to the malleability of the energetic body. Emotional states are literally contagious.

The mind interprets changes in the body as pleasurable or painful. These changes could be the result of internal factors (hunger, illness, etc.) or external factors (environmental change).

The mind also interprets images stored from past experiences and entertains scenarios for the future. While these projections occur in the mind of the individual, they are still able to produce shifts in the body or bodies. The mind is the mediator between our experience of reality and our interpretation of that experience. Changes in the body are interpreted by the mind, and changes in the mind cause shifts in the body. Oftentimes, a situation that happened years ago, or a situation that has yet to happen, will cause more pain than what is happening *here* and *now*.

MIND

The mind has a powerful role to play in our experience of pleasure and pain and is ultimately responsible for our experience of suffering. One, the mind interprets changes in the physical and energetic bodies as pleasurable and painful. Two, the mind interprets changes in the environment as beneficial or harmful. Three, the mind replays situations from the past and entertains possible scenarios for the future, resulting again in changes in the physical and energetic bodies interpreted as pleasurable or painful.

These interpretations, however, are limited to our experience of life (and traits passed down through the evolutionary line). Pleasure and pain are subjective responses to objective stimuli. Pleasure is not objectively "good," and pain is not objectively "bad." The pleasure experienced through drug or alcohol abuse can have drastic consequences, and the pain experienced in childbirth is a part of the miracle of life.

The link between the mind and body is causal and bidirectional. Changes in the physical and energetic bodies are interpreted by the mind, and images projected by the mind cause changes in the physical and energetic bodies. Manifest reality is in constant flux. These changes (changes in the body, changes in the environment, etc.) are neither good nor bad. They just are. Pleasure and pain are mental interpretations of change. These interpretations, however, are limited and almost always accompanied by judgment (pleasure is good and pain is bad).

Our interpretation of reality is based upon the evolution of the human mind, both on a macro and micro level. Macro evolution, the slow development of species since the conception of the universe, has provided modern human beings with the tools necessary to survive in their environment. Micro evolution is the development of an individual being (form) specific to its lived experience (which is the basis of macro evolution). We change as we experience life; and as we change, so does our interpretation of reality. Pleasure and pain are mental interpretations of change. And, these interpretations are limited to the evolution of the mind.

We interpret changes in our body and the environment (as well as images stored from previous experiences and scenarios entertained as future experiences) as pleasurable or painful, and, ultimately, as good or bad. Good and bad are judgments based upon our limited understanding of life. An experience is "good" if I perceive it as beneficial and "bad" if I perceive it as detrimental.

Physical pain is typically judged as bad because it is associated with malfunctions in the physical body. Our perceptions, however, are limited and isolated to the mind. While pain is often perceived as detrimental, it is a necessary component of existing within a body. The physical and energetic bodies are constantly changing, as is the environment within which they exist. Change is neither good nor bad; it simply is.

SUFFERING
Thirst

As judgment is isolated to the mind, the mind is the cause of suffering. Because we judge certain experiences as good and others as bad, we are incessantly trying to increase one and decrease the other.

Buddha taught that suffering is the result of *tanha* (Sanskrit–"thirst" or "craving"). All humans have an innate thirst for goodness. We crave circumstances that we consider good and seek to avoid circumstance that we consider bad. I enjoy spending time with my wife (i.e. spending time with her is good). I, therefore, strive to spend as much time with her as possible, while decreasing our time apart.

Our definitions of good and bad are not limited to the amount of pleasure or pain that we experience. We often strive to increase what is good and decrease what is bad in the lives of others. We work to alleviate poverty, offer our time and energy to friends and loved ones, and join together in coalitions that stand up for the rights of all people. We engage in these activities for the same reason that we exercise or meditate: to increase what we believe is good (health, peace of mind, equality, etc.) and decrease what we believe is bad (disease, poverty, inequality, etc.). Yet, while our intentions are honorable, it is our incessant thirst for goodness that causes us to suffer.

Freedom

The web of existence is a hierarchy of interrelated forms acting and reacting freely. God does not control; God does not coerce; God simply gives. God empties itself into creation as a result of God's sole desire to know itself. We, and all other expressions of God, are free.

Without freedom, life would not have meaning. The reason that your experiences are meaningful is that you are free to experience them. God cherishes every experience you have because God can only experience them through you. Life is a free expression of God. This freedom, however, comes at a cost. One, our experience of life is not always pleasant. Two, life is beyond our control.

The forms that comprise the web of existence are constantly changing (change, after all, is a necessary component of a life), and our minds interpret these changes as pleasurable or painful. The mind also entertains scenarios from previous and future events as pleasurable or painful. Over time, we come to judge certain experiences as good and others as bad. Yet, good and bad are mental interpretations that do not exist outside of the mind. In reality, there is no good or bad; there is just change.

This does not mean that we should cease striving to create as much "goodness" as possible. We interpret certain experiences as good for a reason. We should never tire in our effort to deepen our understanding of what is most beneficial to living beings and help to create a reality that is most conducive to that understanding. We must accept, however, that our understanding of pleasure and pain is subjective and limited. Believing an experience to be good or bad does not necessarily make it so.

Embracing our subjective and limited understanding of experience is the first step to alleviating suffering. The second is letting go of the illusion of control.

Karma

Reality is in constant motion. Our actions are part of that motion. When we act, we participate in the ongoing expansion of life.

Karma is the Sanskrit termed used in Indian philosophy and theology to describe the universal law of cause and effect. *Karma* states that every thought, word, and deed (cause) produces a fruit (effect). We act and there is a reaction. The nature of the reaction (the fruit) is based upon factors that are both internal and external to the acting agent.

Internal factors are determined by the nature of the energy being exerted by the agent. Actions[2] are the result of intention. Intention is the life force of an action and refers to the conscious and unconscious forces that determine the desired outcome—the aim of the arrow, as Buddha would put it.

I walk to the refrigerator to get something to drink. My intention to do so may be the result of thirst rising in the physical body, drink preferences developed over time, and diet restrictions (self-inflicted or recommended by a doctor). These are just examples of the internal factors of which we are conscious. There are a multitude of forces within us that influence our intentions, and most of them are unconscious.

---

2. By "actions," I am referring to thoughts, words, and deeds.

We do have a certain degree of influence when it comes to creating the life that we intend. Many in the New Thought Community refer to this phenomenon as *The Law of Attraction*. We could, of course, just as easily refer to it as the Law of Intention. This law is nothing new, but the result of our ever-deepening understanding of causality. The Law of Attraction focuses on the development of clear intentionality in order to manifest the type of internal energy necessary to create a reality that is "good." Understanding the complex nature of the human mind and bringing to light the multitude of internal factors (conscious and unconscious) that go into determining intention are crucial to personal development.

The more you know about yourself, the clearer your intentions become. But this is only half the story.

We are not alone in creation. Our actions interact with an incomprehensible number of external factors, resulting in the ongoing dance of causality. I am thirsty. First of all, my specific drink preference is the result of an ongoing interaction with the external environment (social conditions, time of year, etc.). Second, there are a limited number of drink options in my refrigerator; these drink options are based upon the availability of beverages in the area where I reside; and this availability is subject to cultural preferences and economic resources. Suffice it to say, the effect (or fruit) created by even the simplest action (going to the refrigerator to get a drink), is determined by countless internal and external factors.

Imagine acting within a reality of innumerable other agents with intentions of their own, and you will begin to understand the complex web of *karma*. We do have a certain degree of control when it comes to intentionality. We do not, however, have control over the outcome.

Suffering

We have a natural thirst for goodness. We interpret change as pleasurable or painful, judge experiences as good or bad, and ultimately strive to create a reality which reflects the most good. We seek to control the past, present, and future. We try to act in a manner most conducive to goodness, and we seek to eliminate those experiences which we consider bad.

Yet, our understanding of goodness is limited to our experience of life, and the vast majority of factors contributing to the outcomes produced by our actions are beyond our control. We can never create exactly the reality that we imagine; and, even if we could, it would be based upon a limited conception of it.

Our efforts to control the past and future are rooted in a limited understanding of goodness. We store images from past experiences and entertain scenarios for the future. We seek to control past experiences by replaying them in our mind. We relive experiences that we consider good and manipulate memories we consider bad.

I cannot tell you how many times I have replayed experiences in my mind, considering the ways in which I could have acted differently. If only I had said this or done that, then the situation would have gone "better."

Our attempt to control the future is similar as we attempt to manipulate experiences that we *may* have. I am going to a job interview tomorrow. *This* is how I would like that job interview to go. Of course, trying to control the past and future leads to the same result as trying to control the present: suffering. We cannot change the past, nor can we relive it. And the future will never match our limited expectations. There are simply too many factors involved.

We suffer because we thirst for goodness. The goodness that we thirst for, however, is limited to our experience of life. There is no way we can truly know what is most beneficial to ourselves and others. The pain that I am experiencing today could lead to abundant pleasure tomorrow. Or maybe the pleasure that I seek will cause others pain.

And, even if we did know exactly what was best for every manifestation of God, we could never create that reality exactly. There are far too many factors involved in the ongoing dance of causality for us to manipulate all of them. Life is a free expression of God, and it is beyond our capacity to understand or control. This is the only dance there is,[3] and it is beautiful.

LETTING GO

In the *Bhagavad-Gita*, Krishna, the incarnation of Vishnu (the God that sustains reality) teaches Arjuna that he must learn to act disinterestedly in order to free himself from the cycle of *karma*. According to Krishna, we are bound by the desired outcomes of our actions. By seeking to control the outcome, we become prisoners of our expectations.

But, what if we had no expectations? What if we acted freely with no thought of return? What if we mirrored God's creative act?

What if we let go?

3. Baba Ram Dass refers to our experience of life as "the only dance there is" in order to signify that it is all that we have.

Krishna teaches Arjuna that if he relinquishes control and gives himself fully to God (Vishnu), he will have peace. If suffering is the result of trying to control reality, when we give up control, suffering ends.

God gives itself freely in the creative act. By letting go of control, we can begin to act freely, thus participating more fully in creation. This does not mean that we should cease striving to know ourselves. Nor does it mean that we should have no intention when acting. Knowledge of the self is crucial to personal and spiritual development. The more we know about who we are and how we relate to God, the clearer our intentions become.

As long as we are bound by our desire to control the outcomes of our actions, our intentions will be misdirected. It is like aiming an arrow at a target with your eyes closed. By giving up control, our intentions become directed outward. We do not love to be loved, we do not give to receive, and we do not create in order to be rewarded. We just give, as God does.

The first step to alleviate suffering is accepting our limited understanding of what is good; the second step is letting go. Seeking to control the outcome of an action (thought, word, or deed) binds us to an expectation that can never be met. Nor would we want our life to become exactly what we imagine. Our greatest potential lies in becoming a full expression of God, not an expression of our limited imagination.

Reaching our potential as manifestations of God does not mean that we will live a life without pain. Pain is a necessary component of existence. For instance, the intense pain experienced as a result of the loss of a loved one is tied to the love experienced through that person. The more we love someone, the more pain we will experience when it is time to let that loved one go. The pain we feel is the result of change.

When losing a loved one, we must adapt to a reality that no longer includes his or her physical presence. Love itself does not change; our relation to it does. Mourning is the process of reorganizing one's conception of reality around the space created by the absence of something or someone that has been an expression of love. Without the experience of love, there would be no need to mourn.

SPIRITUAL PAIN

There is one type of pain that can be alleviated, because it does not actually exist. The spirit body does not change. What we experience as spiritual pain is a perceived disconnection with the spirit body as a result of suffering. The spirit body is always present; our connection to the spirit body cannot be severed. It can, however, be forgotten.

As long as we seek to control reality, we will never fully experience the freedom inherent in God's creative act. God gives itself freely. If we are to be free and become a full expression of God's being, we too, must give freely. Once we open ourselves to the freedom of God's creative act and cease striving to control reality, God's presence will be able to move through us unencumbered. By letting go, we act freely. By acting freely, we give as God does.

Our perception of spiritual pain has its source in ignorance. The world of *maya* (illusion) is constantly changing. The spirit body, however, does not change. Seeking to control reality is like trying to hold onto the winds of a hurricane. The more we grasp for control, the more out of control we feel.

The world of form–the physical and energetic bodies–is motion. Like the eye of the hurricane, the spirit body is stillness. By letting go of the winds, we fall back into the peace of God's being, which is our being. Though the winds still move, creating pleasure and pain, we remain motionless. And suffering ends.

Where is God in Religion?

> Tao can be talked about, but not the Eternal Tao.
> Names can be named, but not the Eternal Name.
> As the origin of heaven-and-earth, it is nameless:
> As "the Mother" of all things, it is nameable.
> So, as ever hidden, we should look at its inner essence:
> As always manifest, we should look at its outer aspects.
> These two flow from the same source, though
> differently named;
> And both are called mysteries.
> The Mystery of mysteries is the Door of all essence.
>
> –*Tao Teh Ching*: Verse 1[1]

RELIGION IS THE RECORD of humanity's ever-evolving understanding of God and creation (limited as it may be). The myths and symbols of religion enchant us, its rituals move us, and the mystics guide us into the unknown. Religion is an indispensable part of the human experience. Though the world's religious traditions continue to evolve, becoming unrecognizable to past generations, the religious endeavor will go on. Every human being who

1. Wu, *Tao Teh Ching*, 3.

encounters God leaves his or her mark on the religious landscape.

Religion proper can be divided into three interrelated spheres of inquiry: spirituality, theology, and religion.

SPIRITUALITY

All that we have come to know about God, along with all that has ever been known, is the result of spirituality. "Spirituality" can be used to describe both the experience of God, or spirit[2], and the conscious pursuit, or discipline, of engaging and deepening that experience. In order to understand the scope of spirituality, we must first isolate it from religious belief. The experience of God precedes descriptions of it, descriptions typically developed within a religious tradition. One does not need to be religious to have an experience of ultimate reality. Nor does one need to refer to that reality as "God."

God is within and beyond all that is. God's eternal being is the transcendent backdrop of creation and the immanent vibration that animates it. We are, therefore, experiencing God always. We are not, however, typically aware of this experience. Most of us are engrossed in *maya*, the illusion that the reality of the senses is all there is. On the other hand, there are certain experiences that provide us with a glimpse into ultimate reality (the eternal reality of God which sustains temporal reality).

You are walking in the woods when you come upon a small pond surrounded by rocks and flowers. You stop and look more closely. There is a beauty in this scene which transcends the particulars of sight and sound. It is

2. From the Latin *spiritus*, meaning "breath of God."

almost as if creation has stopped moving just long enough for you to catch a glimpse of eternity. You cannot describe it; yet, there is something beyond the woods which is far more "real" than the woods themselves. This is a spiritual experience.

Spirituality refers, first and foremost, to the conscious experience of God. If I ask a Christian about her spirituality, she might describe to me an experience of the eucharist (the sacred meal wherein Christians symbolically consume the body and blood of the Christ). I am not asking her to describe what she believes is actually happening during the eucharist, nor am I referring to the ritual itself. I am asking for a description of the experience. Spirituality is the root of the religious endeavor. It is the experience of God which drives our desire to know what God is and how we might live in harmony with God's presence.

The conscious experience of God is life changing. Whatever the catalyst is for this experience (art, music, religion, nature, etc.), we immediately feel that we have been granted access to a more authentic reality. If we are brave enough, we will reorient our lives to serve what we have discovered. What began as an experience becomes a discipline. Our "spirituality" will be the ongoing experience of ultimate reality (whether we call it "God" or not), coupled with our endeavor to serve and deepen it. The musician dedicates his or her life to music, the artist paints, and the teacher teaches. And, as long as they are consciously aware of the reality that is present within the experience, they are spiritual.

There are many paths that one might follow in order to consciously experience the eternal reality of God. As long as you are consciously engaged in an activity that opens you to God's presence, you are spiritual. Many who are spiritual have no desire to understand the source of their experience. It is enough that they engage it. It is enough that they serve it. It is enough that they are changed by it.

Yet, there are others who become curious about the nature of their spirituality. What is this presence that I have stumbled upon, and how does it relate to the reality of the senses? These are the questions of theology and the building blocks of religion.

THEOLOGY

Theology is best described by the words of St. Anselm of Canterbury: *fides quaerens intellectum*, which is Latin for "faith seeking understanding." Faith is *an orientation toward the experience of God which results in an existential certainty of God's existence*. Creation is in constant motion. We experience temporal reality as the rise and fall of interrelated forms. Everything changes and nothing lasts.

When we engage ultimate reality however, we are brought into accord with that which does not change. The spiritual experience opens us to the presence of God within and beyond creation. Our certainty of God's existence (faith) is not an intellectual one. It arises, instead, from the eternal nature of our own being, which is God's being. Experiencing God is knowing God, and knowing God transforms us.

Theology is the process of seeking to understand the faith experience. As we open ourselves to the eternal reality of God's being, our temporal character is transformed. By engaging God, we are better able to express God. And, by expressing God, we come to better understand our relation to it.

Theology is the ongoing dialogue between God and those who seek to know God. The dialogue does not provide answers; it provides descriptions. The words of the theologian are an echo of the spiritual experience. As the individual is transformed, the words of the individual become transformative. The truth of theology is not in the accuracy of its ideas; it's in the presence of God within those ideas.

RELIGION

Religion is the historical and cultural record of humanity's efforts to engage and deepen the spiritual experience. Religion's two primary components are myth and ritual.

Myth

Humans are story tellers. We describe our experience of the world in narratives that help others to understand our perspective (to "see" what we "see"). When you read a book or look at a painting, you are given a glimpse into the reality of the one who created it. Van Gogh's *The Starry Night* is not an objective image of a small village. Instead, *The Starry Night* is the story of how Van Gogh experienced a small village at a specific moment. All humans share their experience of life through narrative. Myths are no different.

Myths are symbolic narratives that recount the experience of God.[3] A symbol references a specific aspect of reality while, at the same time, participating in it. The American flag represents not only the United States, but the ideology upon which it was founded. The American flag is tied to the American experiment. It participates in the reality that it represents and could never be replaced at random.

Symbols are typically used to represent abstract realities like freedom or power. They are necessary for just that reason. They reflect a reality that cannot be qualified. Freedom is an abstract concept. It means different things to different people, and the flag, as a symbol of freedom, is able to participate in each interpretation.

The symbols used to reference the reality of God are particularly important. God is boundless. Thoughts, on the other hand, are finite. We cannot describe God. We can only reference our experience of God with the hope of communicating its transformative influence.

The power of a religious symbol is in its ability to accurately reference and participate in the reality of God. We have an experience of God, and an image arises (typically adopted from our religious tradition). The process is repeated, and if the image works, the experience is associated with it. Over time, the image becomes tied to the reality that it references and will even begin to elicit experiences of it.

For many Buddhists, the image of the Buddha has become associated with the state in which the Buddha lived (nirvana). For these individuals, the image evokes

3. Theology utilizes the same symbols as mythology. It does so, however, in a different format. Theology is descriptive; mythology is narrative.

the experience. The Buddha was enlightened; the image of the Buddha reflects enlightenment.

A myth is a collection of religious symbols arranged in a narrative for the purpose of describing a specific aspect of God and creation. According to the book of Genesis, God created the first human from the dust of the ground and breathed life into him. This is a myth. It does not literally describe God's creative act. It describes an experience of God's creative act.

God's breath moves through Adam, just as God is moving through all of us. The myth is "true" if it evokes a similar experience in us. Creation is a drama. Myth utilizes aspects of that drama to reenact God's creative process. By engaging the story of God and creation, I am able to participate in it. We are storytellers. Mythology is God's story.

Ritual

In order to be transformed by a myth, one must participate in it. A ritual is any activity repeated in order to create the necessary conditions for a desired outcome. Religious rituals create the necessary conditions for a spiritual experience. I read poetry before I write. The ritualized action of reading poetry helps me to create the mindset necessary to reflect on the reality of God.

A myth is a symbolic narrative which dramatizes an experience of God and creation for the purpose of facilitating a similar experience in others. A religious ritual is the enactment of a myth. For example, the eucharist is the enactment of a narrative describing Jesus Christ's relationship to God and his disciples. In the Gospel of Matthew, Jesus is sharing the Passover meal with his disciples (a Jewish ritual). Jesus tells his disciples to eat the bread, which is his body, and drink the wine, which is his blood.

In the Jewish tradition, sacrifices were offered to God in order to atone for the sins of the Jewish people. In the Passover meal, Jesus is offering himself as a sacrifice for those who choose to follow him. In the eucharist, Christians participate in that sacrifice. The disciples experienced God through the life and teachings of Jesus. Christians are able to share in that experience through the myths and rituals of the Christian tradition.

REVELATION

There are many who claim that religious myth and ritual are the result of revelation. Understanding the nature of revelation is key to understanding how religion works. The word revelation means "unveiling." Most of us are caught up in the illusion (*maya*) that the reality of the senses is all there is. Yet, the reality of the senses is merely a veil or curtain hiding ultimate reality.

In the Jewish temple, a curtain separated the Holy of Holies, or Inner Sanctum, from the rest of the temple. The Holy of Holies was the dwelling place of God on earth. God was literally "veiled." Revelation occurs when the veil is lifted and God is revealed to us. It would be a drastic misunderstanding, however, to assume that God chooses when and where to reveal itself. God is fully available to us always. The veil between us and God is an illusion.

We are always experiencing God, but we are typically not aware of it. Our ignorance of God's presence is due to the veil of *maya*. There are certain moments, however, when we are able to see beyond the veil. These are moments of revelation.

For some, God is revealed through dancing or music. For others, God is revealed in the eyes of their children. The purpose of religious myth and ritual is to create the conditions wherein revelation is most likely.[4]

For example, the *Tao Teh Ching* is the revelation of Lao Tzu[5]. This sacred text contains religious symbols that reference Lao Tzu's experience of ultimate reality, which he refers to as *Tao*. The text is a window. Its purpose, like all sacred texts, is to allow others the opportunity to "see" the same reality.

Taoist rituals ceremoniously participate in that reality in order to facilitate the spiritual experience. Lao Tzu's experience of God was so all-encompassing that his entire life shifted in order to accommodate it. Ultimate reality became his primary reality. This is the path of the mystic.

THE MYSTIC

There are many who are able to witness God's presence in specific circumstances. Whether in a temple or in the woods, they return to the site of their revelation in order to experience God again and again. Their experience of God, however, is circumstantial. They rely on specific circumstances in order to elicit the spiritual experience.

The mystic sees beyond the circumstances, experiencing a pure vision of the absolute. The circumstances are seen merely as a catalyst for the experience. Over time, the mystic's experience of God overshadows his

4. Religions utilize elements such as music, art, and nature because of their tendency to aid the revelatory process.

5. Lao Tzu simply means "Old Master." Though myths about its origin abound, we actually do not know who wrote the *Tao Teh Ching*.

experience of *maya*, so that God's presence is experienced within and beyond all things. Jesus told his disciples that the kingdom of heaven was spread upon the earth. The mystic sees it.

The mystic embarks on a journey into the mystery of God. What begins as a vision escalates into an existential longing to merge with ultimate reality.[6] This desire stems from an awareness that temporal identity is merely an illusion (*maya*), whereas one's true identity is God. If the mystic succeeds, he or she will become enlightened.

Enlightenment is complete identification with ultimate reality. The Buddha (translated as "the awakened one"), like other mystics, lived his life beyond the veil of *maya*. Though he moved, breathed, ate, and slept, he remained ultimately aware of the changeless reality sustaining his activities.[7] Change cannot touch the eternal. The one who has awakened realizes this.

There are mystics all around us, men and women who live their lives in the world, but not of the world.[8] The mystics engage temporal reality (though some do withdraw), but do so while completely identified with their eternal selves. To the mystic, life is a dance. It moves and changes, expands and contracts. But, all the while, the mystic remains grounded in that which does not change.

Life moves like the winds of a hurricane. The mystic is the eye of the storm, absolute stillness, absolute peace.

6. In the Greek Orthodox tradition, merging with God is called deification.

7. In the previous chapter, we discussed *karma* as the law of causality. Hindus believe that identification with *karma* binds us in a seemingly endless cycle called *samsara*. *Moksha* is liberation from this cycle and occurs when one has transcended his or her attachment to *karma*.

8. A reference to Jesus's teachings in the Gospel of John.

There are some mystics, however, who share their vision of God with others. These men and women are often called prophets.[9]

Our understanding of God, transmitted through the ages via religious tradition, can never fully contain the reality of God. God transcends our ability to qualify it. Even though religious symbols arise from the experience of God, they are limited to the resources of the mind. In the end, a symbol is merely an idea.

The experience of God pushes religious imagery to expand. The prophet's experience of God is such that no contemporary image will suffice in communicating it to others. The prophet must call upon a new set of symbols in order to share his or her vision. As these new symbols are adopted (meaning they are able to reference and elicit the spiritual experience in others), they become the building blocks for new religious traditions. And, because no symbol will ever serve to convey the full experience of God, there is no end to the evolution of religion.

Our experience of God is the lifeblood of religion, continuously supplying it with new ideas and images. Like all human endeavors (art, government, science, etc.), religion lives and breathes as we do. The prophets, however, experience God in such a profound way that the traditions surrounding them shift dramatically to accommodate their new vision. Historical figures like Jesus of Nazareth and Buddha play a particularly significant role in the ongoing development of religious tradition. They provide us with new paths to walk as we seek to deepen our relationship to the absolute.

9. In Buddhism, they are referred to as Bodhisattvas, beings who have awoken (buddhas), but remain in the world of form in order to help others to awaken.

Yet, these men and women are merely the torch bearers on an endless journey. In the end, we must walk the path ourselves.

THE JOURNEY FORWARD

We are all innately spiritual. As God is both the backdrop of reality and the active principle that pushes it to expand, we are experiencing God always. God does not choose to reveal itself to the mystic. There is nothing in the existential nature of Jesus or Buddha that provided them with "inside information." God is reaching out to all of us. The mystic simply reaches back.[10]

We have all had a vision of ultimate reality. Maybe we caught a glimpse of it while playing a sport (often referred to as being in "the zone"), or perhaps we heard it between the notes of our favorite song. Because God is everywhere (omnipresent), there is nothing that cannot be a catalyst for the spiritual experience. It is our job to pay attention. It is our job to reach back.

The symbols of religious tradition give us insight into the spiritual experiences of the mystics that have come before us. Each set of symbols is a language used to reference the absolute and a map disclosing a path walked by the mystic into the unknown.

Yet, each tradition has its cultural and historical particulars. Jesus was a Palestinian Jew. Therefore, his vision of God was articulated using Jewish imagery. Although Jesus's vision broke free from contemporary Jewish myth and ritual creating a new religious tradition, Christianity

10. Catholic theologian Karl Rahner describes grace as "God reaching out." In the Christian tradition, it was Jesus who reached back.

still bears the marks of Judaism. Each new tradition transcends and includes the traditions that have come before it. To look back through the world's religious traditions is to look into the mysterious face of God through the eyes of the mystics.

No myth will ever fully describe the spiritual experience. The reality of God is eternal, while ideas and images are limited. Yet, we are able to experience the fullness of God at all times. We must look beyond the veil.

We catch glimpses of God all the time. This is God reaching out to us. It is our obligation to reach back, to respond to the call of our eternal nature. When Jesus dies in the Gospel of Matthew, the veil in the Jewish Temple is torn in two. This is a symbol referencing the eternal accessibility of God. The veil is an illusion. There is nothing that separates God from you, me, or anyone. Religion is the record of those who have come to know this.

Where is God in My Life?

> An invisible and subtle essence is the Spirit of the whole universe. That is Reality. That is Truth. Thou art that.
>
> –*Chandogya Upanishad* (6:12-14)[1]

LIFE IS A GIFT. In this moment, *here* and *now*, God is expressing itself through you, as you. Most, however, are not fully aware of the magnitude of this simple truth. Every breath we take, every word we speak, each time we witness the sun rise–these are gifts of God's being.

What would it be like to see reality as an expression of God? If we knew the meaning of life, would it change the way we lived? God is *here* and *now*. It is time for us to see it.

THE MEANING OF LIFE

The meaning of life is to experience it. This simple axiom is both the answer to life's most important question and the method by which we fulfill our potential as expressions of

1. Mascaro, *The Upanishads*, 118.

God's being. All the wonders of creation are the result of God's single desire to know itself. Each individual form that comes into being is unique. Thus, each form represents God's only opportunity to experience life in the manner specific to that form.

You are the only *You* that ever was or ever will be. Your biological makeup, the specific circumstances of your life, and the myriad ways that you respond to those circumstances will never be, and can never be, repeated. God can only experience *your* life through *you*. Your life is a gift given freely by God for a single purpose, to experience it.

To experience life is a given. The act of living presupposes that the one who is alive is experiencing it. Even simple life forms with little to no self-awareness are experiencing life (molecules, trees, earthworms, etc.). Therefore, if the meaning of life is to experience it, then all forms are already fulfilling their purpose as manifestations of God. There is nothing specific that any expression of God need do to receive God's blessing. Life is God's blessing. By experiencing life, you are fulfilling your role as an expression of God. In order to better illustrate this point, let us examine a doctrine from Protestant Christianity.

Most denominations within Protestant Christianity hold to the doctrine that humans are justified by faith. Unfortunately, a good many Christians confuse faith with belief. This distortion of the meaning of faith leads these individuals to conclude that being justified by faith is equivalent to being accepted by God based upon the merits of a specific belief system (i.e., "if I believe that Jesus died for my sins, then my sins will be forgiven."). However, like most religious doctrines, the implications

49

of justification by faith go much deeper than is tradition-
ally understood.

Faith is *an orientation toward the experience of God
which results in an existential certainty of God's existence.*
We are all experiencing God. The person of faith, however, *knows*[2] that he or she is experiencing God. This individual is justified, not because of a specific belief about
the spiritual experience, but because of the certainty that
arises as a result of the experience. The person of faith
realizes that there is nothing that she need do in order to
earn God's blessing. Life is the blessing.

God experiences life through the innumerable
forms in existence. God knows what it is to shine because
of the sun, God knows the wetness of water because of the
rain, and God knows what it is to *be you* because God is
experiencing life *through you*. As you experience life, so
does God.

You are living your purpose simply by being alive.
Yet, being alive does not necessarily entail reaching
your full potential as an expression of God (self-actualization). While most forms reach their full potential
naturally, we have a choice, a choice made possible by
self-consciousness.

SELF-CONSCIOUSNESS

A living being's potential for expression is determined by
countless internal and external factors. An oak tree will
grow to a certain height based upon its biology (internal
factor) and environment (external factor). A squirrel will
gather food, procreate, and play based upon the particulars

2. This is not a cognitive knowledge, but a "knowing" that arises
as a result of the spiritual experience.

of its life. Like most forms of which we are aware, the oak tree and squirrel have not developed the degree of self-consciousness necessary to alter the trajectory of their lives. Their actions are completely determined by factors beyond their control.

This does not mean that they are not free. The oak tree and the squirrel are still expressions of God interacting with countless other forms in a free environment. They cannot, however, reflect on their actions. Thus, they cannot choose whether or not to reach their full potential. Like the majority of other forms in creation, the oak tree and squirrel will merely respond to God's creative impulse, acting and reacting based upon the particulars of their existence. They will reach their full potential as expressions of God because it is in their nature to do so.

We, on the other hand, have a choice.

All forms are experiencing life. We, however, are aware that we are experiencing life, and this changes everything. While our potential as expressions of God is still determined by internal and external factors (biology, environment, etc.), our capacity for self-consciousness means that we are able to reflect upon the experience of being alive.

As I sit here typing, I am aware that I am sitting here typing. I am an expression of God's being and a conscious participant in the miracle of life. And, because I am self-conscious, I have a choice. I can fully participate in my life as an expression of God, or I can live the life that I *believe* is best for me. I can let go and allow God to move through me, or I can act based upon my limited understanding of what is good. Self-consciousness drastically increases our potential as expressions of God, but it also makes reaching that potential an uncertainty.

Each of us is, in essence, trying to live the best life possible (the life with the most good). But, what is "good?" Our understanding of good and bad is rooted in our subjective experience of life (pleasure, plain, desire, etc.) and the subjective experiences of those who influence us (familial values, peer pressure, societal norms, etc.).

Our understanding of goodness and our quest to live the life that is most good are confined by the limits of our understanding. Self-consciousness means that we can reflect on what it means to live a good life and choose to act accordingly. Our potential as expressions of God, however, far exceeds any idea that we can entertain. Our understanding of goodness is temporal; it is based upon our experience of temporal reality. God, as the foundation of goodness, is eternal.

Goodness as a judgment is a mental interpretation that does not exist outside of the mind. Yet, it is grounded in a reality that transcends thought. Like beauty, goodness is a quality that we experience even though we cannot fully comprehend it. We seek goodness because we are drawn to it. Goodness is the quality of an experience or action being of benefit to creation. And, as creation is an expression of God, God is the origin of goodness.

Our problem is that in seeking goodness, we get distracted by our ideas about what is good, ideas that stem from an experience of living (as a task to be mastered) instead of an experience of life (as an expression of God). We must transcend goodness as a judgment and enter into it as a reality. We have a choice–to live our lives according to what we think is good or to become an expression of God's goodness.

People of faith know that they are experiencing God and act in accordance with that experience. Their actions are good, not because they comply with any preconceived idea of "goodness," but because their actions are in harmony with God. And, as their actions are in harmony with God, so too their lives become full expressions of God. Their thoughts, words, and deeds become echoes of God's creative act.

Like all forms, our potential as expressions of God is based upon the specific circumstances of our lives (internal and external). By grounding our actions in the experience of God, we allow God to express itself fully through those circumstances. As self-conscious forms, we are able to witness this miracle unfolding.

The ultimate potential of a self-conscious expression of God is to consciously participate in God's desire to know itself; we are able to know God as God knows itself through us. The person of faith responds to the gift of God's being by accepting and participating in that gift. Self-consciousness means that we have the capacity to reflect on our experiences and act accordingly.

But what if we reflected on our experience of God, an experience that we are all having? What if we sought to know God as God knows itself? Consciously entering into the eternal reality of God is the root of all spirituality. The presence of God's being that sustains our existence is within and beyond all things. It is available to us always. All we have to do is look for it.

SPIRITUAL PRACTICE

Spiritual practice is the process of recognizing and engaging the spiritual experience. We are experiencing God always, but we are often not aware of it. This is due to the fact that our center of awareness is grounded in the reality of the senses.

We identify with what we are aware of and not what is ultimately aware of it. We are under the illusion that our bodies, thoughts, and environment are all there is, so our center of attention remains with temporal reality. We spend the majority of our energy focused on the incessant movement of life and wonder why our lives feel so chaotic. Shifting our attention to God means that we still engage in life, with its ups and downs and opportunities for growth, but we remain grounded in that which does not change. We act in the world, but not of the world.[3]

The first step in any spiritual practice is to recognize situations that open you to the experience of God. Perhaps you feel the peace of God when you are surrounded by nature. Or, maybe dancing brings you into harmony with the ground of your being. For many, the presence of God will be made available during the enactment of a religious ritual. Whatever circumstance brings you into accord with the stillness that is at the center of your life, and all life, this is your pathway to God. And though the particulars of our paths may differ, they are all marked by the three most common responses to the spiritual experience: peace, love, and joy.

Peace

Life is change, and we often become overwhelmed by the movement of it. Not only is the vast web of life beyond our capacity to control or understand, but the sheer amount of data that we are privy to on a daily basis is enough to

3. An interpretation of the words of Jesus as found in John 17:14.

make anyone anxious. Yet, beneath the constant change of creation is the stillness of God's being which supports it. The being that animates our life is God's being, and the consciousness that is aware of our life is God's consciousness.

When we encounter God, our attention shifts from the constantly changing landscape of temporal reality to the peace of God's eternality. When you experience God, however you experience God, you will find that the peace of God's being calms you. Temporal reality is still moving, but you are grounded in stillness.

Love

Our experience of temporal reality is also one of duality (subject/object). You are the subject witnessing the many forms (objects) that rise and fall within your awareness. Even thoughts are objects being witnessed by you, the subject. The primary phenomenon sustaining this illusion of duality is the ego. The ego is the result of your self-consciousness creating and maintaining its idea of *you* as an individual form.

Imagine the ego as a mosaic. The smaller images of the mosaic are the numerous qualities that make you unique (looks, personality, thoughts, emotions, etc.) Arrange all these unique traits into a larger image and you have what the ego considers the unique self. The ego is, of course, a natural and important aspect of self-consciousness. The ability to view ourselves as autonomous individuals is highly advantageous when navigating the world of form. This image, however, is part of the illusion of *maya*.

God's single desire to know itself is the impetus for the creative act. When God divides itself into knower (subject) and known (object), God realizes itself as creation. God is the eternal consciousness (subject), aware of all objects, and, ultimately, the objects themselves. Thus, every experience of life is God knowing God. In fact, creation comes into being for just this reason, so God can know God.

When we become conscious of the presence of God, the illusion of duality breaks down and we catch a glimpse of the oneness of creation. We become the knower and the known, the subject and the object. The recognition of our eternal self in another is the root of love.

And while the vast majority of our experiences of love are conditional, meaning that we recognize a conditional aspect of ourselves (a reflection of our desires, an aspect of our personality, etc.), the spiritual experience opens us to unconditional love.[4] When we experience God, we recognize the core of our being in and through what we are experiencing. We become nature. We become the dance. We are creation.

Joy

The experience of life is joyous. This does not mean that the experience of being alive is always pleasurable (a sensory experience). Nor does it mean that we will always be happy (a frame of mind). Joy is the experience of God emptying itself into life. Joy is, therefore, not subject to the ups and downs of temporal reality. It does not diminish

4. In many relationships, the conditions which supported the experience of love initially break down over time, and the two move deeper into loving one another unconditionally.

with pain, nor can it be extinguished with hatred. Joy simply is.

When we experience God, we open ourselves to the wonder of the creative act. And, as we become aware of the presence of God creating within and around us, we unlock the natural joy of living. Joy is always present, just as God is always present. We can experience joy in the midst of grief, fear, and frustration. The spiritual experience opens us to that reality.

Once we recognize the circumstances through which we are made aware of God's eternal presence, we must choose to engage those circumstances regularly. Spiritual practice is just that, a practice. We have an innate spirituality, just as a musician may have an innate talent. But like a musician, we must participate in the process of honing our potential. We do this by entering into the reality of God, time and again.

We return to nature, we dance, we enact the rituals of our religious traditions. Spiritual practice is a discipline. It requires actively engaging the circumstances that open us to the presence of God. It also requires giving your full attention to those circumstances. Only then will your practice become a meditation.

Meditation

Every authentic spiritual practice is a meditation. Meditation is the practice of bringing your center of awareness in line with the consciousness of God. As we navigate the peaks and valleys of temporal reality, we give our attention to work, family, entertainment, etc. Of course, the more we give our attention to a specific object, the more directed our attention becomes. The center of our awareness is typically located with the object we give our attention to most.

For example, if you are always focused on work, you may find it difficult to focus on other objects when you are not working. This is due to the fact that your awareness is centered on the act of working. Our center of awareness is the hub around which our lives revolve. It establishes and reinforces our primary identity (I am a CEO, I am a husband, I am an actor) and our principle values (power, family, creativity). Our lives are the result of where our attention is directed.

As long as the center of our awareness is located with temporal objects, our state of being will be subject to the ups and downs of living. As life changes, it takes our attention with it, creating turmoil and discomfort. Meditation is the practice of bringing one's full attention to the eternal moment, *here* and *now*. Whatever circumstance opens you to the eternal reality of God, it must be engaged without interpretation or judgment.

As long as you are focused on your interpretation of an experience or your ideas about whether an experience is good or bad, you have not given your full attention to the eternal moment. God is the consciousness that is experiencing life through us (subject/knower) and the being that sustains that which we are experiencing (object/known). God is all that is. Meditation brings one's central awareness in line with consciousness itself by allowing us to see reality as God does.

When we give our full attention to an object or activity without interpretation or judgment, our center of attention drifts back into consciousness itself. Our interpretation of an experience cannot contain the experience itself. Once we let go of our limited understanding of the object that we are experiencing, we become identified with the subject that is experiencing the object. *I am* the one who is walking. *I am* the one who is painting. *I am* the one who is having these thoughts. "I am" is the consciousness that is aware of what we are experiencing.

In the book of Exodus, when Moses asks God his name, God replies, "I Am (Hebrew–*Ehyeh*)." God is consciousness itself. Meditation is the practice of seeing life from God's perspective. It is the process of giving one's full attention to the circumstances through which we experience the presence of God.

The more we repeat our spiritual practice, the more our center of awareness will become aligned with consciousness itself. The circumstances that open us to the eternal presence of God are important. The potential for our experience of God is not, however, isolated to those circumstances. God is in and beyond all things.

We can experience God in all things. As we discover peace, love, and joy in our spiritual practice, we will find that peace, love, and joy follow us wherever we go. Our lives can become a meditation. We can give all that we are to the eternal moment *here* and *now* and come to witness the wonder of creation in all things. As life becomes a meditation, life will also become a prayer.

Prayer

Meditation is bringing one's attention to the eternal presence of God. Prayer is living from that presence. Prayer is acting (thought, word, and deed) in harmony with God. It is expressing gratitude for the gift of life. It is seeking wisdom from the ground of being. And it is choosing to move as God moves.

When we participate in the reality of God's good-ness, our lives become an expression of it. When we give our attention to the *here* and *now*, we act in the *here* and *now*. Spiritual practice frees us from the limitations of what we believe is good and allows us to participate in goodness. The apostle Paul wrote: "Pray without ceasing" (1 Thessalonians 5:17). Prayer is the act of moving from the spiritual experience. And the more we enter into the experience of God's presence, the more our lives will reflect it.

As we engage the eternal reality of God, that reality is expressed in every nuance of our lives. Though we may have little control over the circumstances that make our lives unique, we can allow God to move fully within those circumstances. We have a choice of whether or not we become a full expression of God's being. We can choose to live in accordance with what we believe is good, or we can act from the goodness that is God.

Life is a gift given freely so that God may experience life through us. If we choose to allow the presence of God to be activated in our lives fully, we will become expres-sions of peace, love, and joy.

Life is good, not because the experience of life is al-ways pleasant, but because it is a gift. God is pouring itself into creation *here* and *now*, and as self-conscious forms, we can reflect on the wonder of it. Jesus did not discover the kingdom of heaven because he was existentially differ-ent than you and I, and Buddha did not awaken because he had access to a reality that we do not.

The kingdom of heaven is in our midst, and nirvana is the natural state of one who lives in the *here* and *now* always. Spirituality is a practice of seeing. It is discovering those moments when the world stops and you come face to face with eternity. And, it is returning. God is all there is, and God is *here* and *now*. You just have to see it.

Where is God in the End?

For you are dust,
and to dust you shall return

–Genesis 3:19

WE LIVE, AND WE die. Forms expand as they are animated by the vibration of God's eternal being and contract as being returns to stillness. As manifestations of God's being, our experience of life is brief. Yet, it is brevity that gives life meaning. We are flashes of God's self-knowledge. We *become* so that God can know life through us. This experience is a gift. The gift, however, must be returned.

TEMPORALITY

We experience life as the rise and fall of temporal forms. Each of these forms exists as an expression of God's desire to know itself. God cannot know God as an eternal reality. God's eternality is boundless and, therefore, beyond knowing. Thus, the formless becomes form, and the eternal becomes temporal.

It is the temporality of creation that makes God's experience possible. God *knows* God as God *becomes* bound by the circumstances of its expression. Each form is unique because of its finitude. And, it is because of a form's finitude that it cannot, and will not, last forever.

Unique Forms

Each form in creation is a unique manifestation of God's being. Thus, each form represents God's only opportunity to know itself in the manner specific to that form. It is a form's unique character that makes it indispensable to God. The specific arrangement of internal and external factors that comprise a form's individuality has never been and will never be repeated. You are the only you that ever was or ever will be. Your life is a gift *from* God; your individuality is a gift *to* God. A form's uniqueness, however, is intrinsically linked to its finitude and, therefore, its temporality.

A form is finite because it is bound by the parameters of its unique characteristics, determined by internal and external factors. An individual form is separate from all other forms because of the very boundaries which limit it. I have a set of unique characteristics which you do not. If neither of us had any limitations, there would be nothing to differentiate us. No form can be limitless. A form's limitations make it unique.

A form's potential as an expression of God is determined by its character (the amalgamation of its characteristics). A form's character is unique, offering God a unique opportunity for expression. Yet because a form's character is unique, it is also finite, and so is the breadth of its expression. All forms expand toward a potential limited by their unique character.

We measure the rate of expansion as time. All forms are finite; thus, all forms exist for a finite length of time. Life is finite because it is unique, and life is brief because it is finite. And both make the experience of life meaningful.

Unique Experiences

The quality of this moment is determined by a specific arrangement of forms which has never been and will never be repeated. Greek philosopher Heraclitus is famed for the observation that "It is not possible to step twice into the same river." The countless forms contributing to the uniqueness of this moment are constantly shifting, including the vehicle (physical and energetic bodies) through which we experience it. And because the mind as an extension of the brain changes as the body does, our perspectives change with each new experience. We are continually looking at a new reality with new eyes; we are new individuals stepping into new rivers.

This is your only opportunity to experience this particular expression of the *here* and *now*. Therefore, this is God's only opportunity to experience this moment through you. The temporality of the moment is what makes it so indispensable. And the temporality of all moments is what gives life meaning.

We are momentary expressions of God's desire to know itself. We are *here* and *now*, and then we are gone. God fulfills its longing by becoming finite. Your life is indispensable to God because it is brief.

ETERNITY

We experience life *as* the rise and fall of temporal forms. We experience life *from* the eternal *here* and *now*. Your life is an expression of God. The being that animates your life is God's being, and the consciousness that is aware of your life is God's consciousness.

Creation as an expression of God is finite. God as that which expresses itself as creation is eternal. Your circumstances are continually changing, and your body (energetic and physical) is changing along with it. Yet, your experience of this change is grounded in the unchanging reality of God's being. Life moves; your awareness of it does not.

Heaven

Eternity is *here* and *now*. Creation expands and contracts from the eternal ground of being. The reality of the senses, however, creates a veil of illusion (*maya*). We typically accept that the life of temporal forms is all there is. Therefore, as forms expire, so do we.

The belief that heaven is a separate sphere of existence is actually rooted in the fear that when our bodies die, we will cease to exist. Heaven as a place in time (an extension of the timeline beyond death) is a projection of our desire for an everlasting self (ego). Yet, because the self is a mosaic of the temporal attributes that make each of us a unique expression of God, the self is finite. Heaven is not an everlasting home for the self; it is the eternal dwelling place of the spirit.

Spirituality is the process of shifting one's center of awareness (and, therefore, one's identity) from the temporal to the eternal. You are experiencing life from the eternal *here* and *now*. The shifting forms that surround you (your body included) will eventually fade out of existence. The consciousness that is aware of them will remain.

As you consciously engage the eternal reality of God through spiritual practice, you will fall back into the center of your life (and existence). Identification with form creates fear and anxiety. If you identify with the temporal movement of creation, you will never be settled. Identification with the being that sustains your form results in a life of peace, love, and joy. There is a stillness at the center of your life. You can be that stillness.

Life is change. Mountains crumble, stars implode, and humans die. But we can witness this change as God does, from the eternal *here* and *now*. This body–within which I have experienced so much–will eventually return to stillness. The consciousness that is aware of my body, however, is beyond the temporality of form. As a conscious expression of God's being, I can witness my life expand and contract, appreciating the wonder of it all. I can embrace each experience in its brevity and, ultimately, return the gift that God has given to me. Most importantly, I can fully participate in God's desire to know itself. As God knows me, I can know God.

You are a human being, meaning you are a human manifestation of God's being. In time, the human form will fade. The being, however, remains. All forms come from God, are sustained by God, and return to God. Forms come and go. God remains. You do not go to heaven when you die. You never left.

Bibliography

Easwaran, Eknath. *The Dhammapada*. Canada: Nilgiri, 1985.

Ladinsky, Daniel. *The Gift: Poems by Hafiz*. New York: Penguin Compass, 1999.

Lao Tzu. *Tao Teh Ching*. Translated by John C. H. Wu. New York: St. John's University Press, 1961.

Mascaro, Juan. *The Upanishads*. London: Penguin Books, 1965.

Meyer, Marvin. *The Gnostic Gospels of Jesus*. New York: Harper Collins, 2005.

www.ingramcontent.com/pod-product-compliance
Lightning Source LLC
LaVergne TN
LVHW021620080426
835510LV00019B/2680